Christianity and Other Faiths

CHRISTIANITY AND OTHER FAITHS

An Evangelical Contribution to our Multi-Faith Society

Exeter
The Paternoster Press

AUSTRALIA:
Bookhouse Australia Ltd.,
P.O. Box 115, Flemington Markets, NSW 2129

SOUTH AFRICA:
Oxford University Press,
P.O. Box 1141, Cape Town

British Library Cataloguing in Publication Data

Christianity and other faiths.
  1. Christianity and other religions
  I. Wootton, R.W.F.
  261.2   BR127

ISBN 0-85364-363-6

Typeset by Photo-Graphics, Yarcombe, Nr. Honiton, Devon
and Printed in Great Britain for The Paternoster Press,
Paternoster House, 3 Mount Radford Crescent, Exeter, Devon
by The Pitman Press, Bath

CONTENTS

PREFACE

Of the many changes that have taken place in our society in post-war Britain, the influx of great numbers of men and women from different religions and cultural backgrounds is undoubtedly one of the most significant. Changes inevitably call for adjustments. Slowly, but we trust surely, we are learning to live together and to respect one another. It is a sad reflection on human nature that legislation has to be passed in order to ensure that those of another colour or race are treated fairly. Christian people, at least, should not need any such legislation. We believe in a God who is no respecter of persons, a Saviour who was pleased to talk with a woman of Samaria, even though the Jews would at that time, have had no dealings with Samaritans. John Oxenham sums up the Christian position when he writes:

> In Christ there is no East or West
> In Him no South or North
> But one great fellowship of love
> Throughout the whole wide earth.

However, by writing the words 'in Christ' Oxenham indicates he has the Christian church in mind, a supra-national body of believers made up of 'brothers of the faith'.

The situation we face is somewhat more complex. We have to think through our attitudes towards those who do not profess the Christian faith yet are now our next door neighbours. We are growing accustomed to seeing Muslim mosques and Hindu and Sikh temples springing up in so-called Christian England. This is a situation earlier generations were never called upon to face.

This small book is an honest attempt on the part of a group of evangelical Christians to come to grips with the present situation. All would be one in affirming the uniqueness of Jesus Christ as being the only way to God. None would question his true deity. They would not regard discussion with those of other faiths as "swapping insights". Yet they would agree that we need to know what our neighbours believe and we need to think through our attitudes to such issues as inter-faith dialogue. We trust this contribution will go some way in helping Christians to do just that.

GILBERT W. KIRBY
President, Evangelical Alliance

HOW THIS BOOKLET CAME TO BE WRITTEN

The church in Britain, reeling from its contact with secularism, virtually non-existent in the inner cities, apparently having lost its way and increasingly irrelevant to the masses, has found the encounter with men and women of other faiths to be hard and difficult. Charged with racism and intolerance, misrepresented by those delighting in vagueness and criticised by those of its own members who prefer a meaningless neutrality, it is not only struggling to come to terms with these ideologies but also to rediscover itself, its meaning and relevance to the world and the very foundation upon which it has rested throughout the centuries.

Christians are being challenged afresh to love the stranger and outcast, to seek justice for all men deprived and despised whatever their colour, class or creed and to assert the historic doctrines of the Christian faith with conviction and purposefulness, believing that the power of the gospel will triumph over all difficulties.

It was in this situation that a small group of evangelical Christians was called together by the Evangelical Alliance and planned this booklet. Whilst it recognises the enormity of the issues and so does not seek cheap solutions, it equally strives to give some guidance to Christians living with peoples of other faiths. An evangelical contribution to the debate is vital in the face of so many voices raised in this arena that express a disregard for the biblical record and traditional interpretation. The booklet's underlying assumptions are: that faithfulness to the scriptures must be the guiding light; that integrity and intellectual honesty are of paramount importance; and that compassion must be the ruling force.

The group owes a not inconsiderable debt to Canon R.W.F. Wootton for undertaking the majority of the work both in the writing of the drafts and in the editing of the finished work. Without his efforts this work would not have been possible. It is therefore a matter of special sadness that Canon Wootton died suddenly shortly before this report was published. He is greatly missed.

Thanks must also be offered to the Evangelical Alliance for their sponsorship, support and guidance.

It is in all humility that this report is present, with the prayer that it will be helpful in the formation of a truly Christian attitude towards other religions and in the developing of Christ-like ministries to their followers.

PATRICK SOOKHDEO
Chairman of the Working Group

INTRODUCTION

Gone are the days when the Christian could sing with full sincerity and meaning the words of the familiar hymn:

"In heathen lands afar
Thick darkness broodeth yet,"

implying a division of the world into 'Christendom' (with only a tiny minority of Jewish people) and 'heathen lands'. Today no such distinction can be made. On the one hand, some at least of the 'heathen lands' have been Christianised, in the sense that the majority of the population professes some form or other of Christianity and active church involvement is higher than in many lands of the former Christendom. On the other hand, many of *those* lands have been deeply influenced by secularism or communism to the point at which Christianity has become the religion of a minority. Further, with the immigrations into Western Europe following the Second World War, considerable numbers of people professing other faiths (to whom the term 'heathen', with its derogatory overtones, is no longer applied) have entered those lands, where they now constitute minorities of up to 5%.

Some have come in response to direct invitations, arising from a shortage of labour in the fifties and sixties, some through their own enterprise with the object of improving their economic position, some as political refugees who had no future where they lived before, like the latest arrivals from Vietnam. Some are 'guest-workers' coming for a limited period, not permitted or not desiring to settle permanently, but the majority have made their homes and put down roots in the lands of their adoption; indeed a large proportion (in Britain, for example, about half) were born there and have known no other home.

The greater part of them are Muslims, coming from many lands but especially from Turkey, Algeria, Pakistan and Bangladesh, but there are also a considerable number of Hindus, Sikhs and Buddhists, especially in Britain. They have settled mainly in the inner cities, where they speak their mother tongue among themselves, maintain their old cultural patterns and have their mosques and temples where they continue their traditional worship. At the same time a few of the indigenous population, disillusioned with secularism and lacking contact with vital Christianity, have been attracted to the other faiths, particularly to the mystical side of Islam (Sufism) and to the *guru* sects among the Hindus, some of which have hundreds of European adherents.

The religious situation which has thus arisen cannot be separated (except in theory remote from actuality) from two other aspects of our plural society. One is the purely racial, underlined by a difference of colour and often enhanced by the memory of colonial rule, which makes it difficult for many Europeans to accept the newcomers fully on terms of equality. 60% of a class of children aged 15 in a church-related school in a multi-racial city expressed the view that coloured people were inferior to white people. Many who would never subscribe to such an idea still have in their hearts a racial feeling of which they are quite unaware, which shows itself in avoidance of close contact with black people or in a patronising attitude to them.

The second aspect is cultural: an ethnic community with different language and different customs in respect, for example, of music, food, patterns of family life and relations between the sexes, is looked on as an alien element and often its presence is resented by the indigenous people. Religion is closely bound up with culture, and frequently people who have only the remotest connection with a Christian church are displeased to see the presence of other faiths in their midst.

In consequence of these two factors, attitudes which belittle coloured people, generalising conceptions of how they may be expected to behave (often remote from reality) and feelings of jealousy towards those newcomers who succeed through hard work and frugality are strong in many multi-racial areas, and indeed elsewhere, and some white Christians cannot help being influenced by them. The whole situation has been further complicated in recent years by unemployment and deprivation in many inner-city areas, resulting in bitterness and frustration among the under-privileged (many of them black) and by racist propaganda which has given rise to physical attacks on black people, including a number of racially motivated murders. All these factors are bound to influence any Christian response to the presence of many people of other faiths in the neighbourhood.

While many evangelical Christians have long been aware of this new religious situation, their response to it has been far from adequate. Some, while energetic in their support of foreign missions, have been quite indifferent – or even hostile – to the many people of other faiths in their own city. This is due partly to the inbred racism and colour-consciousness which we have just noticed and partly to the fact that giving to and praying with overseas missions is generally much less demanding than being involved with people of a different culture and background living in the next street.

There have however been some noteworthy exceptions. Some national and some local Christian bodies have been conspicuous in the fight against racism, often making plain the Christian motivation of their action. A number of local churches have worked hard for reconciliation and good community relations in their areas. Some Christian groups, but not generally evangelical ones, have sought to build bridges across the religious divide by promoting the study of other faiths and seeking opportunities for discussion on religious subjects with their adherents who live in the same area. Other churches, mainly evangelical, have engaged in direct evangelism, visiting from door to door, distributing literature, arranging meetings for young people, etc., and a number of people associated with various agencies are working full-time in this ministry.

In this booklet we are seeking to set out a Christian attitude to the people of other faiths around us and to examine the principles involved in relating to them in positive ways and the opportunities and difficulties of sharing with them the life-giving message of the gospel.

1

THE STATUS OF OTHER FAITHS

In assessing the status of other faiths in relation to his own and to God's plan for his creation, the Christian will naturally start with the witness of the Scriptures.

The Old Testament

In the first eleven chapters of Genesis we read of God's dealings with the *whole* of mankind, before the calling out of a special people. We read of his creation of human beings 'in his own image', i.e. with the gifts of reason and conscience and with the capacity to respond to God in a personal way, of his giving them dominion over other creatures, of his provision for their family life, and of their rebellion and punishment. We also read that sin continued in the human race from generation to generation, but that some at least were accepted by God through the means of sacrifice offered in faith (Gen.4:4; 8:20) and that one person, Enoch, for many years 'spent his life in fellowship with God'

(Gen.5:24 GNB). With the great flood, the survival of Noah and his family and the offering by Noah of an acceptable sacrifice, comes the account of God's first and everlasting covenant with mankind (Gen.9:16), a token of God's mercy, a 'cosmic covenant' which was never cancelled or forgotten. This was followed by the event of Babel (Gen.11), speaking once more of human sin and divine judgement. This whole section is vitally important as indicating God's relations with all people, before the call of Abraham and his descendants, with the special covenants which were given to them. Kenneth Howkins's comment (in an unpublished essay) is apposite: 'God has not entirely ceased his gracious activity among men; there is the "common grace" of God operating in the world, preventing it from becoming entirely corrupt.'

The rest of the Old Testament is mainly the story of the people of God, chosen not for their own sake, but to be the channel of blessing eventually for 'all the families on earth' (Gen.12:3). To them he reveals something of his glory and majesty, his mercy, holiness and judgement. He gives them his law, making a covenant with them through sacrifice. Those outside the Mosaic covenant (including of course many descendants of Abraham and Isaac outside the chosen line) mostly figure as the enemies of Israel, who worship false gods, whose customs (which include idolatry and human sacrifice) are abominable to God, to such an extent that close contact with them itself brings defilement and judgement and so is forbidden to God's people. Some writers have sought to tone down the Old Testament denunciation of idolatry on the ground that idol-worship is mainly denounced when it involves unfaithfulness on the part of Israel to their covenant God, like that of an unfaithful wife. But the frequent occurrence of the phrase 'the abominable customs of the nations' (e.g. Deut.18:9) makes it plain that such practices were hardly less blameworthy among other nations than in Israel.

While due weight must be given to this important strand of Old Testament teaching, there are other strands which appear to reveal a somewhat different attitude.

1. *Many individuals among the Gentile nations are shown in*

living contact with God. Melchizedek, king of Salem, presumably a Jebusite, was 'priest of God Most High', and pronounced this blessing on Abraham:

> "Blessed be Abraham by God Most High, creator of heaven and earth.
> And blessed be God Most High, who has delivered your enemies into your power."

Abraham gave him a tithe of all the booty (Gen.14:19–20). Thus Melchizedek earned for himself a place of honour among the types of the Messiah (Ps.110:4; Heb.5:6–11; 7:1–3). Abimelech, king of Gerar (near Gaza) received a message from God in a dream rebuking him for taking Abraham's wife Sarah; he obeyed God, returned Sarah and made a pact with Abraham; his family was healed of barrenness on Abraham's intercession (Gen.20–21). Jethro, a Midianite priest, became Moses' father in law and 'rejoiced at all the good the Lord had done for Israel in saving them from the power of Egypt'. He also blessed the Lord as 'the greatest of all gods' and offered sacrifices to him (Ex.18:9–12). We might look on him as a convert to the true God, but Scripture does not suggest this nor record his circumcision. The prophet Balaam, apparently a Moabite, received messages from God and 'the spirit of God took control of him', so that he uttered prophecies of God's blessing on Israel (Num.22–24), Rahab, the prostitute at Jericho, was spared by the invading Israelites because she protected Joshua's spies (Jos.2:1–6; 6:23), and so she was included in the roll of honour of the people of faith (Heb.11:31). Ruth, a woman of Moab, was drawn through misfortune into the company of God's people and became an ancestor of the Messiah. A widow of Zarephath in Phoenicia fed the prophet Elijah and received a gracious promise from God whereby her family's needs were supplied through a long drought; her child was restored to life in answer to the prophet's prayer (1 Kings 17). Naaman, the Syrian general, believed in God through the ministry of the prophet Elisha, yet stayed within his own community and made no open breach with idolatry (2 Kings 5:1–19). The people of Nineveh in Assyria repented at the preaching of Jonah and were spared from destruction (Jonah 3).

Nebuchadnezzar, the King of Babylon, the worshipper of a golden image, received a vision from God in a dream and acknowledged the Most High God (Dan. 3 and 4). Darius, the Median king, was brought to worship the God of Daniel as 'the Living God the Everlasting' (Dan. 6). Cyrus, the Persian emperor, was called by God to fulfil his purpose by restoring Judah from captivity and is named the Lord's shepherd and his anointed (Is. 44:28; 45:1–7), 'whom he has taken by the hand', and receives the promise, 'I will go before you and level the swelling hills ... I will strengthen you, though you have not known me.'

2. *Gentile nations are declared to have their place in the gracious purpose of God.* Amos reports his action on their behalf as parallel to the great deliverance of Israel from Egypt: 'Are not you Israelites like Cushites to me? says the Lord. Did I not bring Israel up from Egypt, the Philistines from Caphtor, the Arameans from Kir (Amos 9:7)?' They too like Israel are subject to God's judgement (Amos 1:3–2:8). Egypt and Assyria have with Israel a special place in God's plan and one day will be numbered among his people: 'When that day comes Israel shall rank with Egypt and Assyria, those three, and shall be a blessing in the centre of the world. So the Lord of Hosts will bless them: A blessing be upon Egypt my people, upon Assyria the work of my hands, and upon Israel my possession' (Is. 19:24–25). Among many nations God is being worshipped with pure offerings (Mal.1:11 – the context requires the present tense, not the future, and any reference to a wide-spread Jewish dispersion – 'from furthest east to furthest west' – is inappropriate in the 5th century B.C. when Malachi was writing).

3. *The Wisdom literature* (Job, Proverbs, Ecclesiastes and some of the Psalms) *speaks of the divine wisdom and of living one's life in accordance with it without reference to God's revelation to Israel.* It has close links in spirit, content, form and method with similar literature in Egypt. God is referred to as the creator and guide of mankind and the source of wisdom, but not

as the great law-giver and deliverer of Israel; historical allusions are entirely lacking and references to worship are few and far between. In Job particularly we read of God speaking to a Syrian chief ('my servant Job') outside the context of Israel and revealing his majesty and glory to him.

We may conclude therefore that though God chose Israel as his special channel of blessing to mankind, acting powerfully on their behalf and giving them the law and the prophets, he did not confine to Israel his dealings with the children of Adam; he still had his faithful ones in other nations, men and women enlightened by his wisdom, conscious of his majesty and offering acceptable worship to him, though continuing in the traditions of their own people, and others whom he used in various ways, though they lacked a living relationship with him.

The New Testament

Here we are faced with the question: what status does the New Testament give to other faiths in view of the unique and absolute claims made for 'our great God and Saviour Jesus Christ (Titus 1:18) as the one way to God and the one and only Saviour of mankind? For many the answer would seem to be simple. In him alone is salvation (Ac. 3:12), he alone can reveal the Father (Matt. 11:27), no one comes to the Father but by him (John 14:6), he is the one mediator between God and man (1 Tim. 2:5). The gods worshipped in other faiths are non-existent beings (1 Cor. 8:4–6) or even demons (1 Cor. 10:20–21), and their worshippers are really 'godless' (Eph. 2:12). But if the whole emphasis is placed on these and similar passages (of which there is no lack), we are faced with the problem of finding a place in the scheme of salvation for God's ancient people, Israel, and for those other men and women of faith who, as we have seen, were in living contact with him. Clearly they must be included in the scheme of salvation, though it was God's purpose that 'only in company with us would they be made perfect' (Heb. 11:40).

Besides these there are other strands of New Testament teaching which must be taken into account.

1. God's universal revelation of himself, as witnessed in John 1:9, 'the light that enlightens every man'. William Temple comment on this verse in *Readings in St John's Gospel* is apt: 'From the beginning divine light has shone; it has always enlightened every man alive in his reason and his conscience. Every check on animal lust felt by the primitive savage, every stimulation to a nobler life, is God self-revealed within his soul. But God in self-revelation is the Divine Word, for precisely this is what that term means.' Similarly John Stott declares: 'We should not hesitate to claim that everything good, beautiful and true, in all history and in all truth, has come from Jesus Christ, even though men are ignorant of its origin.' But this light is not in itself salvation; light judges as well as enlightens, and 'men preferred darkness to light because their deeds were evil' (John 3:19).

2. While idolatry springs from the rejection of the knowledge of the true God (Rom. 1:20–23), it incurs condemnation in proportion to the light which people have received from God. So St Paul could speak of 'the times of ignorance' when referring to the idolatry of the Athenians (Acts 17:30).

3. God's providential supply of human needs bears witness to people of all races of his goodness and mercy. St Paul tells the pagans of Lystra, 'God has not left you without some clue to his nature, in the kindness he shows: he sends you rain from heaven and crops in their seasons, and gives you food and good cheer in plenty' (Acts 14:16–17). In this way people are prompted to 'seek God, and, it might be, touch and find him; though indeed he is not far from each one of us' (Acts 17:26). Similarly St Paul writes to the Romans of a revelation of God's 'everlasting power and deity' through nature, though people have rejected this knowledge by 'stifling the truth', by refusing to honour him and lapsing into idolatry (Rom. 1:18–23).

4. 'There's a wideness in God's mercy' which exceeds the limits we often place upon it. Peter's word to Cornelius is the clearest testimony to this: 'God has no favourites, but in every nation the man who is godfearing and does what is right is

acceptable to him' (Acts 10:34). But in assessing the significance
of this statement we must bear in mind that Peter goes on at once
to proclaim that Jesus Christ is 'Lord of all' and that forgiveness is
through faith in his name (vv. 35, 43). Further it is clear from the
next chapter that Cornelius and his friends found 'salvation' and
'life' only through repentance and faith in Jesus (Acts 11:14, 18),
even though his prayers and acts of charity had gone up to heaven
(Acts 10:4).

Conclusions

1. *Jesus Christ is supreme over all.* That Jesus is Lord is the basic
confession of the New Testament. That he is Lord of all was
Peter's proclamation to Cornelius and others like him. He is 'the
first and the last, the beginning and the end' (Rev. 22:13). 'In him
everything in heaven and on earth was created...The whole
universe has been created through him and for him...He is...the
first to return from the dead, to be in all things supreme' (Col.
1:16–18). In Jesus of Nazareth the eternal God came once for all
in great humility to dwell for a season in a human life, not in the
mere appearance of a man but as a real human being like
ourselves, yet without sin. He offered once for all one sacrifice
for the sins of the whole world, then rose triumphant, to reign for
ever as King of Kings and Lord of Lords.

2. *No form of syncretism is acceptable to Christians.* In the light
of these tremendous claims no solution which makes Jesus one of
many 'lords' or which acknowledges many paths to God can
possibly be accepted. If this may seem narrow-minded or
intolerant; we must remember that truth in its very nature is
intolerant. Some people are seeking a 'deeper' or 'higher' truth
which would transcend the differences of the religions or a kind of
federation of religions, each acknowledging the truth of the
others and influencing one another by a sort of osmosis, or a core
of religious experience common to all religions. Typical, perhaps,
is the Liverpool parson who recently said, 'Christianity will have
to negotiate a new system of belief with other faiths, a new

understanding of God'. He, like others engaged in such a quest, was ignoring 'the faith which God entrusted to his people once for all' (Jude 3) and the Bible's and the Church's claim for Jesus Christ. These matters are not negotiable–either Jesus is Lord of all or he is not Lord at all.

3. *Other faiths are not devoid of truth.* Our acknowledgement of Christ as Lord of all does not oblige us to think of other faiths as entirely in error. Lesslie Newbigin well says, 'The Christian confession of Jesus as Lord does not involve any attempt to deny the reality of the work of God in the lives and thoughts and prayers of men and women outside the Christian church. On the contrary, it ought to involve an eager expectation of, a looking for, and a rejoicing in the evidence of that work...If we love the light and walk in the light, we shall also rejoice in the light wherever we find it.' (*The Open Secret*, S.P.C.K., p 198). There is much in other faiths which is in harmony with the Christian faith, e.g. the sense of the tremendous majesty of God, so clearly proclaimed by Islam and also by the Bible (e.g. Isa. 40, 1 Tim. 6:15–16), and the love and adoration of a personal God, found in Sikhism and the *bhakti* movements in Hinduism. We can see here the Divine Word enlightening all men, the Word which is Jesus himself; for all truth is his truth. Sir Norman Anderson writes, 'It is, of course, a common experience for a Christian to learn much from men of other faiths – in devotion, humility, courage and a host of other virtues; and it is perfectly possible for him to learn from the teaching of some other religion a lesson he has failed to learn from his own' (*Christianity and Comparative Religion*, I.V.P., p 93). But our glad acknowledgement of this fact must be qualified by our conviction of the supremacy of Christ. At night the moon and the planets glimmer with the sun's reflected light and dispel a little of the darkness, but when the sun rises in all his glory the planets vanish from sight and the moon's light becomes a pallid glow.

4. *There are sinful and demonic elements in all religions.* This was true of Israel – when the high priest entered the holy place, he was commanded to wear on his forehead a plate of pure gold engraved with the words 'Holy to the Lord' – 'Aaron shall take

upon himself any guilt incurred in the holy offering which the people of Israel hallow as their holy gifts; it shall always be upon his forehead, that they may be accepted before the Lord.' (Ex. 28:38 RSV) It was not simply the official leadership of Israel, the Sadducean priests, but the most devout, the Pharisees, who rejected Jesus and demanded his death. Religion itself can easily become the enemy of truth, man's self-protection against the living God. This is evident in tribal religions, witness the ritual murders which occur from time to time. It is true in other religions, witness the clerical regime in Iran, which claims to be God's rule in opposition to Satan. It is true too in Christianity, seen as a historical phenomenon (and that is how people of other faiths view it, and how we are bound, at least in part, to view other faiths): we may cite the horrors of the Crusades, the appalling persecution of Christian by Christian in many eras, the acceptance by Christian leaders of slavery, oppressive wars and the ruthless exploitation of the poor in the past and of racial oppression in S. Africa today. So religion, Christian and other, often results merely in self-righteousness instead of an encounter with God in his holiness and majesty.

5. *People without Christ are lost*, though not precisely as this has been generally understood. The teaching of the New Testament on this subject seems perfectly clear. It would be obviously wrong to interpret Peter's words to Cornelius (Acts 10:34) to mean that for people of other faiths ordinary human goodness and piety earns them salvation, as this would run counter to the whole teaching of St Paul and St John. Those who receive Christ are saved; those who reject him are lost. But what of those who have never really had the opportunity to receive him, because they have never heard the gospel or have been presented with only a distorted picture of the Christian faith? In considering their situation we must bear in mind that judgement is in proportion to light received; Lesslie Newbigin (*The Open Secret*, p.196) reminds us that 'we are warned to judge nothing before the time (1 Cor. 4:1–5)...It is simply honest to refuse to answer the question which our Lord himself refused to answer (Luke 13:23–30).' Sir Norman Anderson examines the question care-

fully (*Christianity and Comparative Religion*, pp.100–107). After referring to the salvation of people in the Old Testament through the merits of Jesus Christ he continues, 'May we not believe that the same would be true of the follower of some other religion in whose heart the God of all mercy had been working by his Spirit, who had come in some measure to realise his sin and need of forgiveness, and who had been enabled, in the twilight as it were, to throw himself on the mercy of God?' He refers to many precious promises made in the Bible to those who seek God and quotes Zwingli's 'somewhat sweeping' words, 'There has not lived a single good man, there has not been a single pious heart or believing soul from the beginning of the world to the end, which you will not see there in the presence of God.' He adds that this view should not lead to any diminution in evangelism; for such people still lack the *knowledge* of salvation, the assurance of sins forgiven, they do not yet know 'the present experience of joy, peace and power, which a conscious knowledge of Christ, and communion with him, alone can bring', and they have no clear message to pass on to others.

Salvation is indeed through Christ alone, won for humanity through the 'one full, perfect and sufficient sacrifice for the sins of the whole world' which he offered upon the Cross; but this does not necessarily mean that it is limited to those who hear, understand and consciously respond in a positive way to his message. There are those too who, like Cornelius, have a sense of loving dependence upon God and a hope in his mercy without ever having heard that message – can we doubt that God's mercy extends to them?

2

CHRISTIAN ATTITUDE AND ACTION

1. Presence

For the Christian Church to be truly present in the multi-faith city (for up to now it is mainly in cities that the multi-faith society is found, though this will not always be so) it is important first of all that Christians should live there. In fact Christians are generally few and far between in the areas where most of the other-faith communities live, and when indigenous people are converted to Christianity they often move into other areas, to be closer to those of like faith or to improve their situation, as they see it. But the Samaritan of our Lord's story 'came to where he (the injured man) was' (Luke 10:33), and Ezekiel tells us how, when God called him to join the exiles in Babylon, 'I sat where they sat' (Ezek 3:15 AV). David Bronnert writes, "The Lord is calling his people to return to the back streets of our inner-town multi-racial communities to establish missionary churches" (*Jesus Christ the Only Way*, ed. P. Sookhdeo, The Paternoster Press, 1977, p 107), and he stresses the need of a "committed and involved presence in the local church life and in the local community".

Such involvement will entail getting to know the people of other faiths as neighbours and friends whose houses the Christian visits and whom he invites to his own home. True, hospitality has some problems in view of the dietary customs of other faiths and cultures, which differ from our own and from one another; but these problems can easily be overcome by discreet inquiries. Often we Europeans fail badly in this matter of hospitality, and the Christians among us do not heed the New Testament commands about it (Rom. 12:13; 1 Tim. 3:2; Tit. 1:8; 1 Pet. 4:9). Travellers in the Orient receive many invitations, even from chance companions on train or bus; but many Asian visitors, including Christians, have returned home after months in Europe to report that they never saw the inside of a European home. We must never forget that we share a common humanity with our neighbours from overseas – we are all bound up together in the bundle of life (1 Sam. 25:29 RSV) – and in many cases a common citizenship too in the country to which we and they belong.

A true Christian presence will entail involvement in community concerns; a person's identity is closely linked with the community to which he belongs, and this is obviously of greater importance to minority groups than to the majority. So the Christian will seek to understand the feelings of the community, to involve himself in its joys and sorrows and to get to know its leaders, and he will be deeply concerned that all its members should be able to live their lives in freedom and dignity, following the cultural pattern which they have inherited. Obviously some adjustments must be made by them to the customs and laws of their new country, but any attempt to persuade them to assimilate fully to the life around is doomed to failure and indeed is wrong in principle. Europeans outside Europe have never even dreamed of following the maxim, 'When in Rome do as the Romans do', and we cannot expect that of those who come to live among us. A young Asian who belongs to a particular family and ethnic group with its own culture and religious life knows who he or she is; where young people have cast off the restraints of family and community (as sometimes happens), they have lost their sense of identity and indeed become lost people, sometimes embarking on a life of crime and immorality.

If the Christian becomes involved in a community, he will at once come up against the issue of race and the problem of racism. It is important that he should understand the biblical attitude to race, to be seen in our Lord's treatment of those of other races (e.g. Mt. 8:5–13; Mk. 7:24–30; Jn. 4:1–14), in St Paul's teaching (Ac. 17:26; Gal. 3:28; Col. 3:11) and in the life of the multi-racial church of the New Testament. He needs then to examine himself to see whether there are any traces of racial feeling or prejudice in his own heart and, if there are, to repent of them. Evangelical Christians have not always had a good record in this respect, as is clear from South Africa and the 'Bible belt' of the USA. If Christians in this situation maintain any degree of paternalistic or patronising attitude, there will be no true Christian presence, for the Spirit of the Lord, who brings liberty in all our relationships, will be absent.

2. Service

The Christian who wishes to be involved with other-faith communities will be concerned to live among them as a true disciple of the one who said, "Here am I among you as a servant" (Lk. 22:27). This will entail practical action along the lines already suggested. While this may prove a valuable and effective preparation for the gospel, it should not be seen simply or mainly as a means to open the door for evangelism. Where people are in social need, are the victims of injustice and discrimination or are facing problems they cannot cope with, this fact itself represents a claim on the Christian's service, irrespective of the evangelistic opportunity which may result. The Son of Man's words to those on his right hand at the Great Assize are sufficient warrant for this: "Anything you did for one of my brothers here, however humble, you did for me (Mt. 25:40; cf 1 Jn. 3:17). However much we may long for people's conversion to Christ, we are to love and serve them *for their own sake*, not just as potential converts.

Some churches in multi-faith areas are already doing a good deal to serve the whole community around them, by establishing

community centres, advice centres, play groups, clubs for un-
employed young people, language classes teaching adults the
language of their new country, and so on, often with the aid of
funds obtainable from various sources. These deserve the support
of evangelical Christians, as also do the secular agencies, such as
community relations councils, whose members include Christians
together with people of other faiths and men and women of good
will without any religious commitment. Much good work is being
done by such bodies, though it is often belittled and derided.
Christians should not stand aside as mere observers or critics but
be actively involved. It is not easy work, as clashes and
misunderstandings often arise; the Christian will need to listen
patiently to the appeals and complaints of the various groups
concerned, to assess the situation carefully and to serve *along
with* the leaders of the other-faith communities, rather than as
one coming from outside to do things *for* them.

One aspect of service in a multi-racial community is to take an
active stand against those who spread racist propaganda and try
to stir up feeling against the minority communities. There are a
number of fringe groups which are very active in this way, and
their efforts have caused much bitterness on both sides and are
largely responsible for the racially-motivated attacks which have
occurred in some areas. At the same time they influence a large
number of people in the majority community, who, while not
committing themselves openly, come to think on racist lines.
Some may feel that to engage in a propaganda war of this kind is a
political activity in which the Church should not be involved. But
it was just this kind of attitude that made most German Christians
stand aside while Hitler stirred up hatred against the Jews,
deprived many of them of their livelihood and eventually herded
them into the death camps at Auschwitz and Belsen. There are
some political issues on which Christians *must* take a stand as
Christians, as indeed did Amos, Jeremiah and other prophets in
their day. A firm Christian witness on this issue of race will make
plain to people of other faiths that Christians really care for them
and are prepared to act for them and with them, even if it may
involve some unpopularity.

3. Dialogue

We must first be clear about the sense in which this much over-used term is being used. Some have pin-pointed a dozen different uses of the word, others have outlined four or five distinct types of dialogue, from 'secular dialogue' which is concerned with meeting everyday human need, to 'interior dialogue' which is about 'experiencing the reality of God in the depths of the soul' with someone of another faith. We shall use the term to refer to inter-religious discussion, in which the participant seeks to listen as well as to bear witness, to understand the other's faith at the deepest possible level, as *he* understands it, as well as to share his own faith with the other at a like level. Something approaching this is seen in Paul's address to the Athenians (Acts 17:22–31). Here he clearly takes careful account of the thinking of the philosophers, especially the Stoics, and by twice quoting from their writings recognises the measure of truth in what they taught. We notice also his action in 'holding discussions daily in the lecture hall of Tyrannus' at Ephesus (Acts 19:9).

Dialogue in this sense demands much of the Christian participant. He will need to 'banish all confessional pride and all feelings of cultural or historical superiority' (George Khodr, *Mission Trends* No 5, p.48). He will need to be fully open to all that is good and true in the other faith. At the same time it is going too far to say, "Complete openness means that every time we enter into dialogue our faith is at stake...The Buddhist may come to accept Jesus as Lord, but I may come to accept the authority of the Buddha, or even both of us may end up as agnostics" (Professor J.G. Davies, *Dialogue with the World*, S.C.M., p.55). This is just not a possibility which will come within the thinking of the Christian, who has acknowledged Jesus as Lord and committed himself to him for ever. Nor will he be willing to follow Professor John Hick's advice (in *Christian Theology and Inter-Religious Dialogue*, Macmillan) and move from 'purely confessional dialogue' to the truth-seeking stance in dialogue" in the hope that 'each may be helped towards a fuller awareness of the Divine Reality before which they both stand.' True, he will realise that he has barely touched the fringe of the wonder of God's riches in Christ and that (as we have already seen) he may learn something of divine truth from a man of another faith, truth which, though contained in Christian faith, has not fully dawned upon him so far. But he cannot lay aside his convictions when he enters on dialogue and approach another faith as if he recognised it to be of equal validity with his own.

Some have felt that to engage in dialogue at all is somehow to compromise one's Christian faith. However the Uppsala statement of the World Council of Churches (1968) says plainly, 'A Christian's dialogue with another implies neither a denial of the uniqueness of Christ, nor any loss of his own commitment to Christ, but rather that a genuinely Christian approach to others must be human, personal, relevant and humble.' And the Lausanne Covenant (1974) commends 'that kind of dialogue whose purpose is to listen sensitively in order to understand.' It is supremely through dialogue that the Christian can show himself to the other person to be utterly genuine and humble, loving and sincere on the level of personal relationships. In dialogue we are not dealing with religious systems as abstractions; we are dealing with individual human beings who share many of the same hopes and aspirations, the same longings and fears which we have and at the same time confess another faith. We need to learn what makes the other's faith so precious to him, what Islam for instance means to the Muslim who would gladly give his life for it, something far different from what we pick up from newspaper reports of affairs in Muslim countries. In becoming man Christ identified himself with us in our human condition, with all its weaknesses and limitations; it behoves us to come as close as we possibly can to the other person at the level of personal faith – this is the way of humility and love. On the other hand 'the refusal to enter into dialogue often rests on fear, anxiety and overdefensiveness' (A.C. Thiselton, in an unpublished essay).

Further, dialogue has a close relation with communication. Much that we say to people of other faiths simply fails to be understood. Someone has pointed out that the accepted translation of John 3:16 in the language of a Buddhist people would be understood by them as follows: 'God had such a desire for this evil world of continual death and rebirth that he gave his only Son, so that anyone who was credulous enough to believe in him should not be blotted out but go on being born in one body after another for ever.' The Christian speaks of God's Son; the Muslim thinks at once in terms of ordinary conception through physical union and cries 'Blasphemy!' The Christian says one thing; the other person hears something quite different, and there is no real communication. But in dialogue we may patiently learn how our words are heard by the other, and so gradually discover how to make our meaning plain to him, taking account of his standpoint and presuppositions. Such dialogue, according to the Lausanne Covenant, is 'indispensable to evangelism'.

This raises the question of the relation between dialogue and proclamation. The Chiang Mai Consultation of 1977 on 'Dialogue in Community' refused to see 'dialogue and witness as standing in any contradiction to one another'; it accepted dialogue not as an alternative to mission but as 'one of the ways in which Jesus Christ can be confessed in the world today'. We may agree that there is no conflict between them; we do not have to choose one and reject the other. But can dialogue be looked on *simply* as a means to evangelism? A Christian who takes this view will expose himself to the accusation of insincerity and manipulation. The participant who is not a Christian comes to the dialogue (it is presumed) with an open attitude, ready to give and to receive, eager to share what his faith means to him and to listen intently to whatever the Christian has to say to him. If he comes to realise that he is being 'got at', that the Christian is simply using a new technique of evangelism subtly disguised, he will at once be repelled, feeling that he is being exploited and manipulated. The Christian must come *with all sincerity* to listen as well as to speak, to learn as well as to teach, if he is really true to the Lord he serves and the message he seeks to impart. At the same time he will not be surprised if his engaging in dialogue does serve the cause of evangelism, nor will he accept the view, widely canvassed in some quarters, that the *only* verbal approach that the Christian should make in the present situation to people of other faiths is that of dialogue – the obligation to *proclaim* the message still remains.

4. Proclamation

The duty of the Christian to share the good news about Jesus with his neighbour, be he Hindu, Muslim, atheist, agnostic or simply indifferent to religion altogether, need not be argued here. The booklet *Relations with People of Other Faiths* (British Council of Churches, 1981, p.12), leaves no doubt about this:

> 'If we have grasped (or been grasped by) something that is true, the experience is not something which we should keep to ourselves. For the first Christians it was not something they *could* keep to themselves. To treat the story of Jesus as if it were merely private and personal would have robbed it of its public, universal importance, and reduced the Church to a cult of like-minded cranks...The first Christians...wanted the Good News taken to every person.'

The question is: how is it to be done? Clearly there must be no attempt to pressurize or manipulate, for that itself would contradict the spirit of the gospel. Instead there must be that persevering and painstaking effort to communicate whose importance we noted in the last section. The aim is that people may really grasp the message of God's wonderful love and mercy in Christ not only with the head but with the heart and may respond to it as free persons. For this we have to approach people as they are, with a real understanding of their thought-forms and presuppositions as well as of the basics of their faith. E.J. Sharpe is an unpublished essay ('Comparative Religion and Communicating the Gospel', p 12) has expressed this well:

> 'The Christian Gospel is addressed to people. And anyone in whom that Gospel is a fire in his bones or an ache in his heart must first of all become an expert in the study of people. Not in the shape of their heads only (though that may have its place),

but supremely in the secret thoughts of their hearts. And that...is what religion, in all its forms, is about. About men on the verge of the unknown. About men in the grip of fear, panic and awe. About men dancing for joy that spring has come again. And if it is these things which make men what they are, and if it is through these things that men are to be known *as they are* – not as what we would have them be – then comparative religion has a great service to perform in lifting a corner of the curtain, or loosening a brick from the middle wall of partition in the name of Christ who broke that wall down.'

This is just what St Paul is doing in the address to the Athenians, where he takes the thought-forms of Stoicism, even quoting Stoic authors, and seeks through them to open people's minds to the Gospel. Some may call this pre-evangelism rather than proclamation proper. If this is so, it is no less vital to the task, and who can doubt that Paul would have gone on to preach the gospel fully if his audience had been willing to hear him out?

At the same time the channel of communication across cultures must not be allowed to distort the message itself. As Lesslie Newbigin has said (in an address to the annual meeting of the British and Foreign Bible Society):

'Certainly an effort must be made to use the thought-forms of every place and time – whether animist or marxist, idealist or existentialist – to communicate the Gospel. But the language of the Bible retains a certain transcendence over all these necessary efforts, and must control and judge them. Above all, no re-formulation of the Christian faith can be accepted which does not retain at its centre the dominating figure of God, the living God, the God who speaks and bids men answer, the God who acts and by his mighty deeds sets the terms of all man's doing, the God – in other words – of the Bible.'

So for the Christian in Europe today who seeks to share his faith with his neighbours of other faiths, the task of proclamation, though of paramount importance because of our Saviour's commands and the urgency of the message, is not to be seen in isolation. It is to be seen as arising naturally from the situation where Christians are present in hope and love and prayer alongside people of other faiths, where their love is "not a matter of words or talk" but is "genuine and showing itself in action" (1 Jn. 3:18), in the form of costly service on behalf of and in fellowship with the stranger in the midst, where love also leads them on to a real meeting on spiritual terms in dialogue with their neighbours. This may take time; it certainly cannot be rushed. When this is done, or when at least some clear steps have been taken in this direction, then the Christian may hope to be able to communicate the Gospel of redeeming love to his neighbour of another faith. The outcome he must leave with God.

3

PRACTICAL PROBLEMS

1. Inter-Faith Worship

In March 1981 an 'Observance for Commonwealth Day' was held in Westminster Abbey in the presence of Queen Elizabeth II and many dignitaries of Christian and other faiths. It consisted of hymns, readings from the scriptures of different faiths, affirmations about humanity, justice, love and service, and nine prayers and blessings by various religious leaders; so it was clearly an act of inter-faith worship. Such events are not infrequent at a less exalted level.

Evangelical Christians will have little hesitation in rejecting worship of this kind for several reasons:

1. It is shot through with contradictions, because of the radically different conceptions of God and fundamental beliefs among the different faiths. Thus in the Westminster service, for example, God is called 'Father' (something quite unacceptable to the Muslims present), while reference is made to 'gods' and to the transmigration of souls.

2. It is bound to give the impression, whether true or false, that the Christian participant accepts the other faiths as equally valid with his own.

3. It conflicts with the task of evangelism which Christ laid upon his Church.

4. It cannot fail to cause great perplexity in the minds of Christians converted from other religions and any who are weak in faith.

While we deplore public services in which Christians and people of other faiths engage in worship together, it does not necessarily follow that circumstances can *never* arise where it would be right for Christians to engage in prayer with people of other faiths. Thus at Asian funerals Christian ministers have sometimes felt that no principle was sacrificed by accepting a request to pray aloud along with leaders of other faiths; and at week-end dialogue conferences between Christians and Muslims times of intercessory prayer have been arranged in which both faiths participated.

If Christians desire to draw as close as possible to their friends of other faiths at a religious level, are there other ways of doing so open to them than explicit inter-faith worship? The heart of a religion is to be found in its worship – just to *talk* about it is not sufficient. It is natural therefore that some way should be sought (beside that of verbal dialogue) for the Christian to enter into the innerness of another faith and to encourage people of other faiths to draw near to the heart of Christian faith through Christian worship. St Paul envisaged a situation where an outsider might be so affected by witnessing Christians at worship that 'he will fall down and worship God, crying "God is certainly with you!" ' (1 Cor. 14:25).

One way then is for a Christian to visit centres of worship of other faiths and to observe the people at their worship. Indeed this would seem to be essential for a deep understanding of the faith in question. But he will go of course as an *observer*, not as a participant, and avoid any action that might give the impression that he was participating fully. Not all other-faith worship is open to outside observers – thus Ismaili Muslims do not admit outsiders to their worship, though they are open and friendly in other respects and will gladly show their place of worship to visitors. Sunni Muslims (who form the great majority) generally welcome visitors to their mosques at the time of prayer as well as at other times, but this is not the case everywhere; restrictions are sometimes imposed, especially on women visitors. Hindus generally welcome visitors at all times, as do Sikhs, who (like the Jews) provide the head covering which is considered essential for reverence and sometimes supply a meal after the service. The leaders of all the faiths are happy to explain the worship and answer questions; sometimes Sikhs will even invite a Christian visitor to address their Sunday congregation. A visit by a church group to a place of other-faith worship helps to build a friendly relationship, and may be reciprocated, though less often by Muslims than by others. Such a return is an excellent opportunity for evangelism as well as for cementing friendship.

Sometimes meetings between the followers of different faiths are arranged where those of each faith have their own slot with items of their own choosing – a reading, a prayer a song or perhaps a dance. Here many Christians may feel that they can join in with a good conscience, as worshippers during the Christian section of the service and as observers for the rest of the time. Others however may feel that this type of function is open to the objections already mentioned against thorough-going inter-faith worship.

In many cities there are inter-faith councils which arrange events of this kind and also other meetings and discussions between people of different faiths. These certainly provide a good opportunity of meeting devout people of other faiths, of learning from them and of witnessing to one's own faith from time to time. The professing Christians involved in this kind of council often appear to have a universalist doctrine and to be too ready to recognise the validity of other faiths as equal to that of Christianity. Provided that they are seen to be entering such councils in order to learn and to witness to their own faith, evangelical Christians may have a useful place in such gatherings.

2. The Use of Church Property

In many areas where people of other faiths live in large numbers, there is a scarcity of buildings where people can assemble for social, cultural or religious purposes. In some cases the other-faith communities have been able to acquire their own places of worship, adapted or purpose-built, which can also serve other needs, but this is not always so. Sometimes in the same area there are a fair number of churches with halls and other ancillary buildings which are not fully used by Christians as the church is weak in that neighbourhood – we are not referring to the house of prayer itself where the word of God is preached and the sacraments administered, which will be reserved for Christian worship. If the Church is to show the love of Christ in action and to serve the *whole* community around, it would seem natural that such properties should be made available, on loan or hire, to other-faith groups which need them, unless of course there are Christian groups, such as West Indian churches, which obviously have a prior claim. But many Christians will not agree about the rightness of helping other-faith communities in this way.

Where it is a question of purely social and cultural use, most would agree that such hospitality is a Christian duty, on the basis of the general obligation to love one's neighbour and also the special injunction, 'You shall love the stranger as yourself' (Lev. 19:34). Such action may well be seen as holding out a helping hand to people in need and thereby building bridges of friendship with other-faith communities. But what use is *purely* social and cultural? A Hindu wedding reception normally goes along with the religious ceremony, which involves walking round the sacred fire and making offerings (through a Brahmin priest) to the pictures or images of the gods. A 'mother-tongue' language class is often accompanied by instruction of the young in the religion of which that language is the normal vehicle and would involve, in the case of Muslims, for example, an explicit denial of the deity, death and resurrection of Jesus. Some would feel however that the duty of loving concern and action on behalf of others outweighs the disadvantage of appearing to countenance on

Christian premises activities associated with other faiths.

Where however, the use of church buildings is requested for specifically religious purposes, the observance of a festival, regular worhip or religious instruction, a much more difficult question is raised. Many Christians feel that to allow such use is to give the impression of such an alliance with another faith as would impair Christian witness to the absolute claims of Christ and the work of evangelism and would also cause perplexity to many Christians. Such a feeling would certainly be justified if the group in question carried on direct propaganda against the Christian faith, offered worship to statues or pictures of their gods, or sought to win converts from the indigenous population. But where this is not the case, some Christians would be willing to concede the request.

3. Inter-Faith Marriage

The term 'mixed marriage' is misleading, as it is sometimes used of marriages between Roman Catholics and other Christians and of inter-racial marriages where there is no difference of religion (to which there can be no objection from a Christian standpoint, though the social and cultural problems which may arise should be given due weight). We are considering simply those between Christians and people professing another faith.

On this question St Paul makes it clear that while a marriage contracted before conversion should if possible continue when one partner becomes a Christian (1 Cor. 7:12–16), once a person belongs to Jesus Christ he or she is not at liberty to marry outside the community of Christ's people: 'Do not unite yourselves with unbelievers; they are no fit mates for you. What has righteousness to do with wickedness? Can light consort with darkness? Can Christ agree with Belial, or a believer join hands with an unbeliever?' (2 Cor. 6:14–15). It is surprising that Christian ministers sometimes agree to conduct such weddings, and the practice sometimes followed of a Christian service of 'blessing' after a civil marriage is also unsatisfactory.

When two people are contemplating a marriage of this kind, it is the duty of a Christian pastor or fellowship to counsel the Christian solemnly against it. The main appeal will be to the scriptural principle just mentioned, but it will be justified also to refer to the likely social and cultural consequences, especially in view of the plural marriage which Islam permits. Thus Muslims, already married in their country of origin, have occasionally gone through a form of marriage in a European country, without divulging this fact to their new partner, or after marrying for the first time in Europe have contracted a second and quite legal marriage in a Muslim land. There is also a greater likelihood of divorce. Further, strong pressure is often brought to bear on the Christian partner (generally a woman) to embrace her partner's faith or at least to cease any open observance of Christian practices, and to allow her children to be brought up in the father's faith. The other partner will often be obliged to act more as a member of a family than as an individual, because in Asian and Muslim marriages the families are closely involved.

If, in spite of counselling, a Christian insists on contracting a marriage with someone of another faith, the pastoral responsibility of the Christian minister or fellowship with which the Christian partner is associated does not come to an end. It is not their task to cut off that person from fellowship and to have nothing to do with him or her. Rather they should seek to maintain a pastoral relationship and help the person to be loyal to Christ in other respects, even though they have failed in this respect, to meet the problems arising from the marriage, to continue with Christian worship and to strive for the Christian nurture of the children and the conversion of the other partner. They should also seek to make peace within the affected families, and if possible between them; for serious conflicts and bitterness often arise.

4. Education

Education takes place within a social, cultural, political, religious and philosophical framework. Western society is in a state of flux, motivated and modelled by forces from within and outside. The addition of people of different faiths and cultures adds further pressures – positive and negative. Schools today, particularly in urban areas, are secular, co-educational, (and comprehensive?), with a wide range of nationalities, cultures and faiths represented among both staff and pupils. The multi-faith school is a representative slice of society. Schools, as products of Wetern civilisation, accept and convey a vast 'hidden curriculum' of Western thinking about Man, the purpose of life, relationships, truth, the value of education, freedom, authority and so on, which is rarely questioned or openly taught but which underlines and influences everything that takes place.

All education is based on value-judgements which reflect the commitments of the educator. The nature and content of education will be moulded supremely by the educator's view of the nature of man (See Philip May, Lion, *Which Way To School* (1972)). Western society holds conflicting views on this.

He is variously seen as an animal, the highest being in all creation, a child and servant of God, and a cosmological accident. Vast and complex sets of educational philosophies and practices have been built around these and other views of man. The piles of comparatively new but obsolete text books on school shelves serve as silent monuments to past educational trends. It is also comparatively common to find one school department vigorously pursuing one philosophy while another advocates a conflicting policy.

A common assumption in schools is that education is intended to create independence – to make a person 'stand on his own two feet'. Yet this sharply conflicts with beliefs about man's need of dependence on God and with the Sikh emphasis on brotherhood, Christian beliefs about the interdependence of individuals in the Body of the Church, and the fulfilment which the Muslim can find only in the *umma*, the community. In short, the conflict is between the religious framework and the Western secular individualism on which the state school is based.

Two options appear to be open to those who disagree with the state system. First, to set up sectarian schools funded and staffed by the religious group. Secondly, to accept the reality of the state system and seek to transform it at local and national levels. Different Christians are passionately committed to each of these options. More will be said later about sectarian schools, but Christian parents and teachers who choose to remain within the state system will discover a new and challenging dimension to their role as 'salt' and 'light' in the world.

Christian Teachers

Christian teachers frequently find the multi-faith school a more stimulating environment than the school dominated by one cultural or ethnic group. Christians may also experience a greater affinity with staff and pupils, who, whatever their religion, share their religious framework for life, than with others who, despite their Christian cultural background, have a materialistic view of life. Pupils will also be delighted to find support from a teacher who considers religion to be a vital ingredient for everyday life. The Christian teacher may find himself developing a mediating role between secular staff and pupils and those of a different faith in an effort to overcome ignorance, bigotry and prejudice and to generate understanding, tolerance and harmony.

Supremely, the Christian teacher must demonstrate his faith in the quality of his teaching. When Christianity is seen not just as an extra-curricular activity but as something which transforms the whole of life, the Christian teacher will be marked by a concern for truth and integrity in his work, a view of colleagues and pupils as people with value, rights and dignity, and a recognition of his task as a God-given responsibility. (See *Which Way To Teach*.) Frequently, because of the scarcity of teaching posts, in-experienced teachers find themselves in multi-faith schools often in inner-city areas. These schools may contain a small minority of pupils from Christian backgrounds. The young and insecure teacher may see himself as the final representative of Christianity making a last desperate stand against 'heathen' forces. But, in the midst of the traumatic beginning of a stress-laden career, if the Christian teacher can rely on the supreme power of the sovereign God to fulfil the divine role of leading man into truth, then the teacher can enter into something of the joy of teaching in this environment.

Evangelism

It needs hardly to be said that in the multi-faith context evangelism of a captive audience in the classroom is morally indefensible. Outside the classroom, activities aimed directly or indirectly at evangelism should be undertaken thoughtfully, and with the full awareness of the social and cultural consequences of conversion to Christianity. It would seem logical that any opportunity offered to Christians to share their faith should be available to others to do likewise.

Assemblies

Many people have questioned whether a compulsory act of worship is possible, and, if it is possible, whether it is an acceptable activity for a school. Clearly multi-faith acts of worship are impossible in school. The use of such basic terms as 'God' and 'prayer' have such different meanings in different religions that the activity becomes of little meaning, save to inculcate the equal validity of all faiths. Schools faced with this predicament may present an act of Christian worship (in accordance with the 1944 Education Act) and allow dissenters to withdraw. However, this is divisive for the school community, and assumes a commitment to Christianity on the part of the majority–which may well be an erroneous assumption. Another option is to view assembly as an educational activity rather than an act of worship.

This concept may allow those of different religions (and non-religious philosophies) independently to declare their beliefs, demonstrate an act of worship or celebrate a festival, with the rest of the school as observers/listeners. Themes may be adopted for assemblies and religious insights gained by contributions from various religions. This can prove illuminating but runs the risk of syncretism or confusion. Also, where some shared human experience is the theme – love, hate, death etc. – the search for a consensus view may reduce everything to the lowest common denominator. Perhaps the most radical option (expressed by J. Hull in *School Worship, An Obituary*, S.C.M., 1975) is to see assembly not as a 'sacred' occasion but as a central activity in the school, illuminating and integrating the learning process by drawing out common themes from subject syllabuses as assembly material. However these activities are viewed, it is clear that Christians have some radical thinking to do in the area of school worship in the multi-faith school.

Christian Schools

The state educational system, despite absorbing more than half of local government expenditure, is in a state of shocking decline. Examples of excellence abound, but so do horror stories. Many people question the role of education in the moral decay of the nation (the West?). In this situation Christians may well look for alternatives to the ailing secular humanistic state school.

One well-established alternative exists – the state-aided church school. Historically, the secular state education system grew out of the churches' educational activities. State aid given to church schools is a demonstration of the democratic right of parents to send their children to sectarian schools which seek to nurture children in a particular Christian belief system. In our pluralistic society it would be logical to extend state aid to other sectarian schools, to allow parents of all religions their democratic rights. So we could have Muslim schools and Rastafarian schools, among others, supported, at least in part, by rate-payers.

The desire for separate education on religious or philosophical grounds may have serious implications for the very nature of society. In Ireland we see a policy of separate development for two religious groups. Catholics and Protestants have different – and frequently contradictory – views of society and of the past, present and future. A system of 'parallel nurture' exists which builds alienation into the fabric of society. Dialogue, though technically possible, for many is inconceivable. The natural consequence of this example in multi-cultural Britain would be separate development for religious groups (and, by implication, cultural groups) with, for instance, different parts of the inner cities becoming the 'homelands' of ethnic minorities. Is this the type of society Christians want to see?

Another alternative to the state system is the independent sector – for those who can afford it. There appear to be two types of independent Christian school – the traditional independent school with a Christian foundation, and a 'new breed' of school, like those of the Accelerated Christian Education movement, which offer a modern 'radical alternative' to the secular state school.

When the state school system is in such an unhealthy condition; when attitudes to religion are frequently negative; when Religious Education is boring or badly taught or so concerned about objectivity that it misses the very heart and substance of religion; when Religious Education degenerates into Social Education, it is hardly surprising that Christian parents are, perhaps for the first time, thinking about alternatives.

There is no universal agreement about what constitutes 'Christian education', so what can a 'Christian school' expect to provide? What significant difference would there be between a Christian and a non-Christian curriculum? A Christian perspective on Geography would be enriching, focusing on 'God's world', stressing the need for stewardship of resources and so on. It would also pose intriguing questions – why are predominantly Christian countries most heavily involved in the pollution and exploitation of the environment, and why are there rich Christians in a hungry world? Christian studies in History and Sociology would include both descriptive and prescriptive information and would have much that is negative as well as positive to say about the role of the Church. However, one may ask how Christian Mathematics would differ from other types. Some so-called Christian Mathematics courses pathetically include the counting of crosses as though this transformed the subject. Would a Christian mathematician acknowledge our indebtedness to Greek and Muslim mathematicians? Would the Christian scientific method be any different from the method of the non-Christian scientist?

Christian schools can certainly provide Christian teachers, and Christian parents may be comforted by this potentially influencial relationship. However, Christian commitment is no guarantee of teaching ability, and an inept Christian teacher may be a more destructive influence than a competent non-Christian teacher. When considering teaching methods, would it be assumed that the teaching methods of the Lord Jesus Christ would be employed? Or that his methods were superior to those of Muhammad or Shri Guru Nanak Dev Ji? Significantly, however, the critical enquiry method, on which Western education is built, is consistent with Bible injunctions to search and examine (Acts 17:11), to consider (2 Tim. 2:7, Mt. 6:26–30) and to test and discriminate (1 John 4:1), unlike Muslim education, where the truth of the Qur'ān is something to which one submits, without enquiry.

Christians, and others, reject the elevation of man, and the ultimate authority given to human reason, in the humanistic state education system, and seek fresh perspectives. The Christian school can therefore provide a fresh vision of a society based on justice, love and truth, and an environment where, for instance, the belief that *All Truth Is God's Truth* (the title of a book by Arthur F. Holmes I.V.P., 1977) is a basic premise for education. It is easy in this environment, however, to create a 'hot-house' climate which fails to prepare pupils for life in the world, and this may be counter-productive.

There is obviously a great deal of positive Christian thinking to be done about the nature and role of education and its implications for the multi-cultural society. Three questions (at least) require urgent investigation:

1. Is the 'nurturing' of children in a particular faith actually 'education'?
2. Do Christians want a society in which sectarian schools are run by different religions as an alternative to the state system?

3. Should Christians set up Christian schools, particularly as a means of safeguarding their Christian heritage in a multi-faith society?

These issues are interwoven with others – the nature of the child, responsibilities of parenthood, the role of the Church in education and so on. Christians must also ask how they fulfil their responsibilities to God in the society and the world in which they live.

The idea of Christian schools is very attractive. They provide biblical perspectives for pupils, security for parents and purpose for teachers. One may question, however, whether Christian parents can justify withdrawing their influence and their children, and Christian teachers withdrawing themselves and their talents, from the world, in the light of the following words of Jesus.

'My prayer is not that you take them out of the world but that you protect them from the evil one...As you sent me into the world, I have sent them into the world' (John 17: 15, 18, NIV).

Indeed it would seem crucial that Christians fulfil their mission of representing Christ in the world by exerting their influence to the full within the state school system.